BLOCKCHAIN

An Exhaustive Guide To Learning Blockchain Technologies

Adrian McNulty

© Copyright 2018 by Adrian McNulty - All rights reserved.

It is not legal to reproduce, duplicate, or transmit any part of this document in either electronic means or in printed format. Recording of this publication is strictly prohibited.

Table of Contents

Introduction 7

Chapter 1: What Is The Blockchain 12

Chapter 2: History Of The Blockchain 21

Chapter 3: Reasons To Use A Blockchain 27

Chapter 4: The Blockchain In Detail 34

Chapter 5: Potential Applications 47

Chapter 6: Blockchain Projects 55

Chapter 7: Blockchain Security 61

Chapter 8: Future Of The Blockchain 74

Chapter 9: Blockchain Platforms 82

Conclusion 99

Introduction

This book serves as an overview of blockchain technology.

In **Chapter 1**, we will look at what a blockchain is at its most basic: how blockchain transactions work, how different levels of privilege and permissions work, how a blockchain is structured, and how a blockchain is built up and appended to. We will also look at a blockchain's general purposes and reasons why one might use a blockchain.

We'll examine the history of the blockchain in **Chapter 2**. We will see the types of databases, ledgers, and data trees that existed before blockchain, and we will see how variants of these systems were implemented in the blockchain. We will also learn how the blockchain began with the advent of cryptocurrency -- in particular, how it all began with Bitcoin. Finally, we will look at the ways in which recent advances in technology are making blockchains more ubiquitous and how these advances are making transactions more trustworthy and secure, while also providing an open and anonymous system.

In **Chapter 3,** we will see the reasons that a blockchain may be used in a business setting, and we will look more deeply at the reasons for use that we saw in Chapter 1. We will see how blockchains can be used to perform transactions involving money and digital assets, and we will also look at how blockchains can be used to keep and manage records. We will also see how blockchains can provide transparency by only making private data that needs to be private, and how privacy is enhanced by setting permissions that restrict participants from viewing and editing particular information (or permit them to do that). Lastly, we will see how the blockchain can provide a continuously running network that is always available.

We'll study the technical underpinnings of the blockchain in detail in In **Chapter 4**. This is the only technically complex chapter, and it builds on the ideas in Chapter 1. It explains why the blockchain works the way it does by explaining each of its components and why they are so important and useful.

In **Chapter 5** and **Chapter 6**, we will see potential applications of the blockchain, as well as actual projects and startups that people and groups have created. We will discuss projects in areas such as accounting, land registration, fundraising, insurance policies, the sharing economy, government, and record keeping. We will also look at business- and commerce-related projects like data storage, finance, and supply chains.

In **Chapter 7**, we will look at blockchain security issues, and we will see how the blockchain has both advantages and disadvantages compared to traditional systems. We will see not just how decentralization benefits security, but also the particular vulnerabilities that decentralized blockchains have, and how inadvertent centralization can occur. We will also see how small networks can be a risk early on in the life of a blockchain, and how the security of individuals can be compromised even when a blockchain remains secure.

In **Chapter 8**, we'll imagine the future of the blockchain, and how it will evolve from its current use and grow out of being dominantly used by the cryptocurrency market. We will see that blockchains will change business practices by increasing fair competition while also costing less than current systems. Then we will look at how blockchains will change society by providing better options for customers and product distributors and service providers -- essentially building an economy that anyone can participate in.

Finally, in **Chapter 9,** we'll find out about platforms that you can run a blockchain. We will look at major players like Ethereum, IBM's Hyperledger, and JP Morgan's Quorum. We will also look at less well-known but easy to use software like Domus Tower Blockchain, Monax, Hydrachain, Waves, BigChainDB, Chain Core, Corda, Multichain, OpenChain, Symbiont Assembly, and Credits. The chapter will briefly explain each tool and describe the cases in which each is a good choice. We will also look at Docker, which makes it easier to install several of these tools on your server or computer.

Chapter 1: What Is The Blockchain

In this chapter we will examine the blockchain at its most basic. We will see what it is, what it does, and why it works. Some of these concepts will be built upon in later chapters, but for now, let's look at blockchain in a nutshell.

Blockchain In A Nutshell

The blockchain is probably best known as the technology that cryptocurrencies (such as Bitcoin) are based on. But in fact a blockchain can serve a far greater variety of purposes. A **blockchain** is, broadly speaking, a decentralized, permanent ledger of data or assets. The blockchain traces the transfer or exchange of those assets, and by extension, it traces the transactions between its users.

Blockchains can be used to perform all the same transactions that any other system would allow, but the blockchain has the added benefit of being faster, more reliable, more open, more secure, and less costly to administer than typical options. Individuals would once have to manage records of their transactions and interactions manually, and build up their own network of trust.

For example, your bank may keep all of your debit transactions on file, but may only provide the last few months or years of transactions through their web interface, meaning you either have to continuously download your transaction record, save all of your bank statements, or visit the bank to get a detailed record. But in a blockchain, all of these records would always be visible to you immediately, reliably, and securely.

Furthermore, certain users would need to have certain privileges and permissions to oversee and approve the transactions before the transactions were completed. But in the blockchain, all of this authorization and trust is done in the ledger. In other words, in a blockchain, the data is doing the work of the people.

How It Works: Consensus

There are a few things that a blockchain relies on in order to provide these features. First of all, there must be a **consensus**, which means that everyone using the blockchain must agree on how the blockchain works. When there are disagreements, the blockchain may be forked. This may sound risky, and you might think that a group of people can reach a false consensus, but this is almost never the case. The blockchain provides incentives for individuals to reach a consensus that is legitimate.

Consensus also means that the ledger must be shared yet unchangeable: everyone looks at the same ledger, and if an error is made, the error is not overwritten -- the blockchain is instead updated and appended.

The precise mechanism of consensus is optional. There are a few factors which guarantee consensus. **Proof of stake** is one: the users must have something invested in the blockchain's operation. This alone isn't enough, but paired with other features, proof of stake determines which participants collectively have the power to reach a consensus.

Proof of work is another consensus mechanism, in which various participants' machines compete to solve mathematical problems (or "puzzles") and the first to solve the problem have a say as to what version of the blockchain will be used.

Proof of work is frequently used in cryptocurrency and other public blockchains, but using computers to reach a consensus is inefficient if you are using a blockchain semi-privately. So if you are creating a blockchain in a business setting, the blockchain will probably more heavily rely on a proof of stake mechanism or use a unique mechanism.

Finally, note that consensus is automated, and it is not something that end users will typically be dealing with.

How It Works: Decentralization
A blockchain also must be distributed, meaning that the participants are collectively responsible for running the network. That is perhaps the most crucial quality -- it's what makes a blockchain tick, and we will examine it in more technical depth in later chapters. For now, let's

look at how the distributed qualities of the blockchain affect the operation of the blockchain at the user level.

A blockchain ledger is **distributed**, which means that since the people using it are responsible for agreeing upon its function, it can have different levels of privacy and openness. Since no participant has total administrative privileges, nor the ability to make unilateral decisions -- only the data is privileged -- this also means that the ledger doesn't have to be privately viewable, although it can be.

For example, you are not supposed to give your credit card number to untrusted individuals, because it is trivial for them to charge you for more than you agreed to spend. Yet you must give out the credit card number if you wish to spend money – it is semi-public. But in a blockchain, the information used for sending is private, and the information used for receiving a transaction is public. In other words, in the blockchain, you can choose to have some information private, but still have a way of validating that private information without knowing it. This is done through the use of cryptography and one-way functions.

There are various levels of privilege and participants that a blockchain may have. The most basic is simply a user, which covers any participant that has any access at all to the blockchain. Regulators may have special privileges to oversee the transactions and interactions in a blockchain. Developers program the blockchain and program smart contracts. Network operators have special privileges that allow them to create and manage a blockchain. Finally, certificate authorities issue these various privileges. Note that these participants are not necessarily people; they can be automated computer systems as well.

How It Works: Structure

Just as the name suggests, a blockchain is called a blockchain because the data is stored in "blocks" that are chained together. There are two parts: the **block header** (which links each block to the one before it) and the **transaction data** (which is basically just the content of the block, either the data it contains or the value it holds).

Hashes are short strings of text that serve as identification. For every block there are at least two hashes: one hash serves as the block's own ID, and the other is the hash of the previous block in the chain. These unique identifiers are what make a blockchain immutable and tamper-evident.

Multi-signature is a very simple consensus mechanism. It just involves a majority of the blockchain's participants agreeing on a version of the blockchain. This alone is not effective for public blockchains such as cryptocurrencies, but in a business' blockchain with reasonable trust, it can be very efficient.

Why Do We Need It?
We need the blockchain because it has several advantages over traditional systems. Here are a few times when we might need or want to use a blockchain.

When we carry out transactions. Blockchains manage the exchange of assets and finances. These do not have to be financial transactions, though. They can also be transactions of data, items, documents, credits and tokens, software, or just about anything. The blockchain can make anything, even copyable data, into a unique object of value.

When we use contracts. We can (at least some of the time) eliminate the need for a third party that oversees and knows when to carry out contracts. We can replace the third party with a smart contract that automatically runs under certain circumstances, leaving us only with the need to perform audits on occasion.

When systems are costly or time consuming. As noted, blockchains reduce the cost and hours of labour needed to run other systems by removing the need for people to administer the system at all. (However, this must be balanced with the overhead cost of implementing the automated system.)

When there is information that can be made public or semi-public. Cryptocurrency blockchains are famous for being as public as possible, but you do not need to make all of your private information available to all of the blockchain's participants. You can (1) give some participants privileged access to the private information and (2) use cryptography to restrict other participants to access public information and verify private data without actually knowing any private information.

When a system is prone to human errors or attacks. A secure blockchain can be easily audited precisely because it is a comprehensive record of all the activities in question. Illegitimate changes can be detected easily because they are reflected immediately in the blockchain. Errors can be corrected without losing track of the original errors, because no data needs to be overwritten or erased.

Chapter 2: History Of The Blockchain

In this chapter, we will look at the history of the blockchain, starting with its precursor, the Merkle tree. Then we'll move on to Bitcoin, the first blockchain. After that, we'll see how recent developments (sometimes referred to as "Blockchain 2.0") have the potential to automate functions of our society.

Before Blockchains

Before true blockchains, there were systems and concepts that resembled components of the modern blockchain. One ancestor of the blockchain is the Merkle tree, which is similar to a blockchain in that it is a tree of nodes containing data. Every node is dependent on a connected node, which means that, just as in a blockchain, tampering is noticeable -- you cannot change just one node or block without also changing the others.

One main difference is that while a blockchain is immutable (changes are appended), in a Merkle tree nodes can be modified and deleted. Whereas blockchains are decentralized -- there are participants that are all attempting to reach a consensus on the validity of the blockchain -- Merkle trees are centralized. Merkle trees have a root node that determines the validity of the other nodes. More simply put, to say that the Merkle tree is centralized means that the Merkle tree determines its own validity.

The difference is not clearly defined, as blockchains also use a type of Merkle tree. The main difference is that once a Merkle tree's node is changed, the root node should change along with it -- the root is dictating the validity of the tree. In a blockchain, if a block changes, that is a sign that something is wrong -- the rest of the chain should not change -- consensus is dictating which new blocks are added to the end of the chain.

Digital Currencies And Cryptocurrencies
Bitcoin was the first use of a blockchain. Since Bitcoin, there has been a rapidly growing trend of digital

currencies built on a blockchain. Some, such as Litecoin, have merely remained derivatives of Bitcoin. Some have been based on original blockchains, like Monero, which intends to be more private than Bitcoin is.

Others, like Ethereum, have attempted to break away from the cryptocurrency sphere. Ethereum attempts to be a more general-purpose blockchain that can be used to create self-executing smart contracts and to be used for distributed computing. Ethereum just happens to be useful as a cryptocurrency as well.

Only time will tell whether future blockchain projects will be seen as secondary to cryptocurrencies, or if blockchains can thrive independently of their cryptocurrency-focused history. For semi-private blockchains with limited uses in a business setting, there may be little use for cryptocurrencies. That said, for blockchains targeted at the general public, having some tradable asset (or **token**) as part of a blockchain is an advantage in attracting investment. It is unlikely that cryptocurrencies and tokens will go away anytime soon.

Blockchain 2.0

Blockchain 2.0 is a loose term rather than an actual version of any blockchain technology. Essentially, it means that new blockchains are increasingly made to be more tightly interwoven with other technology and trends. It's analogous to the term "Web 2.0" which originated when websites started to interact with each other's content rather than merely exist as simple pages of information. One blockchain 2.0 technology that we've already covered is **smart contracts,** which are blockchain contracts that automatically execute under certain conditions.

dApps are another blockchain 2.0 technology. These are simply computer programs or web applications that interact with the Ethereum blockchain. Metamask is a browser plugin that allows you to run Ethereum dApps in your Chrome or Firefox web browser. At github.com/ethjs/examples you can see examples of these applications, such as a dApp that allows auctions to be conducted.

Decentralized autonomous organizations (or **DAOs**) are another possibility under Blockchain 2.0. Currently, people must enforce the rules and operation of an organization, but with a blockchain, smart contracts could be used to conduct business and manage employees without the need for human administration or management.

What This Means For Society

The existence of blockchains mean that we can have more certainty and trust in our day to day activities. People are faced with difficult decisions, and are sometimes under-informed, no matter what side of a transaction or interaction they are on.

Bettina Warburg explained in a TED Talk that "blockchains lower uncertainty and (...) they therefore promise to transform our economic systems in radical ways (...) I want to go through three forms of [uncertainty] that we face in almost all of our everyday transactions, where blockchains can play a role. We face uncertainties like not knowing who we are dealing with, not having visibility into a transaction and not having recourse if things go wrong."

Sometimes you do not know who you are dealing with, and sometimes you are not sure if your transaction is made in good faith. But blockchains, by serving as a complete, transparent record, mean that people can make completely informed decisions before acting. That said, the blockchain is in its early days, so there is a long way to go before this becomes universal.

Chapter 3: Reasons To Use A Blockchain

In this chapter, we'll look at several good reasons to use a blockchain. They're excellent when it comes to performing transactions, keeping records, providing transparency, and limiting user permissions. They can do everything that a traditional system can do and more.

Performing Transactions

Currently, financial transactions are the premier use of blockchains. In an ideal blockchain, one that is well-designed and that is widely adopted, transactions are cheaper and faster than in other systems, for various reasons that we will see throughout this book. Briefly, blockchains reduce the need to pay high rates for oversight of transactions, and in fact may eliminate the need for overseers altogether. As a result, there are typically low (or even zero) transaction fees that the participants must pay.

Transactions on the blockchain are also more stable and secure, as they give less power to a middleman, although it is possible to appoint an escrow agent on one's own terms if desired. Compared to a service such as Paypal or a bank, which act as middlemen with enough power that they can arbitrarily block or reverse payments, blockchains leave participants much more free to perform transactions as they wish. On the blockchain, a far greater amount of transactions is possible. When it comes to transactions, blockchains provide the freedom of cash, but without the limitations of physical space that make long-distance cash transactions difficult. In short, it's possible to allow anyone, anywhere to participate.

Keeping Records

A blockchain can be used to keep records -- but not surprisingly, blockchains are typically being used to keep records of financial assets at the moment. But here is how record keeping works. Each block represents a transaction, and the creation of each block is encrypted and tied to another block, making the record of the transaction immutable. This permanency makes it easier to audit the records, because records can't be deleted, and because an improper change can be immediately noticed and traced -- the blockchain is transparent and is constantly being examined by the systems that participate in it.

But the blockchain isn't just for keeping records of transactions. It can also keep records of any other interactions or assets. Recall that in a blockchain, any change or deletion will be reflected in another block on the chain. Factom is one blockchain that is designed especially for recordkeeping and auditing. It could be used to prevent government workers from deleting emails when the law demands email records, for example. The record-keeping process can also be tokenized, so that participation in and compliance with the blockchain gives you something of measurable value that you can exchange.

Providing Transparency

A blockchain is typically transparent, which means that anybody can see and inspect its content. This is possible because some of the data is private and encrypted, and other data is public.

Cryptography contributes to transparency by ensuring that only the data that needs to be encrypted is encrypted. Traditionally, when you use a centralized service, some authority has the duty to keep your data protected and keep it from being tampered with or made public.

This would be done by giving the company somewhat arbitrary and unrestricted access to data. In theory, if your credit card company knows all of your private spending habits, it can recognize when someone has stolen your card and is using it in ways that you would not. Of course, if the company knows all about your spending patterns, an outsider could steal that information as well.

But instead of trusting one person with a lot of information, you can trust many people with a little information. That is how the blockchain works. It is safe to let people see any one of your transactions, because those transactions alone are meaningless in terms of identity, and nobody but you has your private information.

Distribution and decentralization also contributes to transparency by ensuring that no single participant or central server is responsible for any data. If the data is tampered with, it will be corrected by the other participants almost immediately in most cases. If one computer or server crashes, or is merely shut down, another will host a copy of the blockchain. No single participant has the responsibility of deciding whether the data has been kept secure, nor does any one participant have to keep the data from being hacked or stolen. "Keeping all of your eggs in one basket" is no longer necessary.

Limiting Permissions

Some blockchains are entirely public, while others are permissioned. Bitcoin is an example of a public blockchain, in which miners and coin holders and other participants can join and leave the network as they like.

There is no need to prove one's identity or privileges to merely view or build onto the network. Everyone is equal: everyone is participating in reaching a consensus for the blockchain.

This works for some purposes, but, naturally, in a business setting you may not want customers and outside agents from participating in the same way that your employees and team members do. So on some blockchain platforms, it is possible to create permissions that limit what participants can see and do. **Ripple** is an example of a cryptocurrency that uses a permissioned blockchain, limiting some types of participation (namely validation of the blockchain) to organizations, such as MIT and Microsoft, in an attempt to bring in participants who hold more value than the typical Bitcoin participant. Ideally, limiting participation to businesses will make Ripple more appealing to financial institutions.

In other words, blockchains will hopefully be taken more seriously in the business realm if they are somewhat limited to actual businesses. **R3 Corder** and **Hyperledger** are two permissioned blockchains that you might use in business settings, and these will be discussed further in Chapter 9.

Chapter 4: The Blockchain In Detail

In this chapter, we will look at some of the more technical features of blockchains, building on what was covered in Chapter 1. For now, recall that a blockchain is basically a database or a ledger that does not have a central authority, and which nobody has total administrative privileges or control over.

Typically, each participant has ownership of some blocks, and the ability to see some or any of the other blocks. Also recall that a blockchain is self-administrating and self-governing, and that the role of participants is not to run it, but to reach a consensus on the correct version of the blockchain.

Blockchains And Distributed Ledgers
The terms "blockchain" and "distributed ledger" are nearly synonymous. The term "blockchain" refers to the

structure and connection between the blocks, just as the name suggests. In a blockchain, the blocks are always in a sequence. Each block consists of a block header, which is simply a reference to the previous block in the chain. The block also consists of "transaction data" -- basically, the data that forms the content of the block.

"Distributed ledger" is a somewhat broader term than "blockchain." Blockchains are by definition distributed ledgers, but there are other types of distributed ledger. IOTA is a token that uses a "tangle," a type of distributed ledger that is more like a network of blocks rather than a chain, where there is no sequence of blocks. In IOTA, any given block's data does not unilaterally depend on another block like it would in the blockchain; instead, each block depends on several other blocks in no particular order.

Decentralized Systems vs. Distributed Systems

When it's said that a blockchain is decentralized, that means that there is no central server. This is in contrast to a centralized server, which is solely responsible for administering the network and for storing all relevant information. In a decentralized system, there is not just one but several servers which may provide dedicated storage, but those servers will not necessarily each hold all of the data, nor will they have total control over the network.

Distributed systems are similar to decentralized systems, in that there is no central authority. However, in a distributed system, there are no servers and no dedicated storage at all. There are no servers, just peers that hold some or all of the relevant data.

That said, there is quite a lot of overlap between the two terms, and they may be used interchangeably at times. Most blockchains are both decentralized and distributed. Furthermore, the term "decentralized" can be used in everyday language to mean that a blockchain is not owned or controlled by anyone in particular -- in contrast to a bank, which is typically run and owned by a single entity.

Peer-to-Peer Systems
In distributed systems, participants must know about the existence of all of the other participants, and

participants must also know about the trustworthiness of the other participants. This may be referred to as a problem of integrity. A technical failure means that each participant can be prevented from having the information that they need. A failure of trust means that someone can exploit the system or otherwise attempt malicious actions.

Together, these issues are called the Byzantine General Problem, which is a thought experiment in which a number of generals must cooperate and coordinate an attack on a city. The problem is that each general does not know whether one or more of his fellow generals are planning to betray the others and lead them into a trap.

The blockchain solves this technical problem by having each participant hold a copy of the blockchain. Because of this, blockchain are typically peer-to-peer systems. This is closely related to the concept of decentralization. A peer to peer system is made up of nodes, and each node exists to create new connections, keep existing connections active, and distribute new information. Peer to peer networks are sometimes called "gossip" networks because they spread information by ensuring that every node that receives information forwards that information to all its peers, and that those peers do the same, over and over again.

However, there are drawbacks in a peer to peer system: if the system is not thriving and is underused, the arrival of a transaction is not guaranteed, and transactions may not arrive in the same order they are sent. Indeed, slow transactions are becoming a problem in older cryptocurrencies such as Bitcoin, and the fees to prioritize a Bitcoin transaction are high.

But at any rate, peer to peer systems solve the technical problem of systems failure or shutdown, because no one participant is responsible for keeping the blockchain alive. For this reason, in a blockchain, each participant or "node" ideally will have an entire copy of the blockchain, although this is not always feasible. If it does, it is usually called a "full node."

Ownership

Let's return to the problem of trust and malicious intent. By now, it should be clear that the blockchain solves the trust problem by making as much information public as possible without sharing private information. This is such a major draw of blockchains, in fact, that blockchain platforms will often boast that they are "Byzantine General-proof." As we proceed through the remainder of this chapter, we will see just how blockchains strike a balance between private and public information.

Even though anyone can publicly view a block in a blockchain, owning a block is a different matter altogether. It's a little like browsing items at a store: you can pick up any item from the shelf, but you need much more that that to prove that you've purchased that item, even though the item doesn't change once you've bought it. In short, then, ownership is all about identifying a participant as an owner, identifying an object to be owned, and linking those two ideas.

The blockchain has several components that make up ownership. Identification data is one, which is simply a unique public ID that shows who you are. Authentication is another, which is the opposite: authentication stops others from claiming to be you. Authorization is a combination of identification and authentication: it is the process of gaining access and control over what you own.

Ownership is important, because once a blockchain can handle ownership, it can be used not just to see who owns what, but also to transfer ownership of assets and data. Thanks to this feature, the blockchain can handle information such as the amount of an asset that is being sent, the time frame in which to perform the transaction, the fees that the owner must pay to the system, and proof that the sender agrees to the transfer. More generally speaking, the blockchain can identify the owner by making use of hashes, which is what we will look at next.

Hashes

Hashes are the IDs that a blockchain uses to achieve ownership. A hash is simply created by an algorithm that produces a short string of text from a large amount of data according to a set of mathematical rules.

There are a few features that the hashes must have in order to be unique.

- Since they are based on data, a hash must be **deterministic**: that means that, if the hash is taken from the same data twice, the hash should be the same each time.

- The opposite should be true as well: hashes should be **collision-resistant**, meaning that if you take the hashes of two different pieces of data, the hashes should not be the same.

- More generally, hashes must be **pseudorandom** so that the same hash doesn't come up twice.

Once these features are achieved, it's also crucial that hashes are **irreversible** one-way functions. If you know the input data and the hash to begin with, you should be able to match the two. But if you know only the hash, you should not be able to reverse-engineer it to find the input data that produced it.

However, in actual fact, if the algorithm is simple enough and the input data is short enough, it is possible to reverse a hash into a number of possible inputs. For this reason, mining is a major part of cryptocurrency blockchains, which involves discovering sufficiently difficult hashes. The effort put into "hashing" or mining is basically a cost for having influence in the consensus-making process.

For the purposes of the blockchains that you might use, though, it's enough to know that hashes are useful for several reasons -- not just proving ownership of a block. For one, they are useful for comparing data without having to compare the entirety of the data. By extension, hashes can also be used to prevent users from accessing outdated information, by creating a sort of "broken link" once data is changed -- but still retaining the data. Hashes are also useful for noticing and detecting changes immediately in a blockchain, because if each hash depends on the previous hash, one change can disrupt the entire chain.

Types Of Hashing

Also know that different platforms will offer different types of hashing, and different types of hashes will be appropriate in different situations. Consider the difference between independent hashing and repeated hashing. **Independent hashing** is the most straightforward, and it's just the hash of some input data, as we've discussed.

Repeated hashing involves taking a hash of a hash, which, as we've also just seen, is useful in creating a chain in which each block's value depends on the value of the one before it. Again, this makes it immediately noticeable when a change is made.

Combined hashing is simply the process of combining data before taking a hash from it. This is useful when the pieces of data are very small, because on a large scale, each hashing process can take a significant amount of time and computer power. Hierarchical hashing is a similar method that is even more efficient method that can be used if the data that is being combined is the same size.

Sequential hashing occurs when new data arrives, that is, when a hash is taken of the new data and the old hash. This is useful in tracing back a hash to the time when it arrived.

Cryptographic Security

The blockchain is primarily made secure through the use of cryptography. As noted earlier, blockchains keep a balance of private and public information, and use hashes to -- amongst other things -- define ownership of each block. You can also look at the distinction between public and private as the difference between seeing and transferring the data in a block.

The bottom line is that you will have at least two hashes for each block. One is a public address that allows people to send data to the block. The other is a private key that allows you to send data from the block that you own. Sometimes, in asymmetric cryptography, you'll have two private keys -- one to encrypt data, and one to decrypt data, which lowers the risk of a security problem, because you are (hopefully) less likely to have both keys stolen.

Blockchains And Centralized Systems

Often, blockchains are decentralized, yet they can be connected to a centralized system. The reason that decentralization is so important is that in the case of a centralized system, the system is only as strong as its weakest point.

This type of security flaw is common in online wallets and exchanges: they are centralized exchanges that store large amounts of cryptocurrency. They do not have any extra security simply because they own something that originated in the blockchain. Mt Gox is one exchange that was attacked in this way, causing millions of dollars worth of Bitcoin to be lost amongst Bitcoin holders.

Meanwhile, the Bitcoins of those who did not use the exchange remained safe thanks to the decentralized blockchain. Since online wallets and exchanges are not an essential part of the blockchain, we can still say that the blockchain is decentralized. In other words, if compromising a single node in a system can compromise an entire system, it is no longer a decentralized system -- and this is almost never the case with a blockchain. Almost all security breaches will affect several users, but not the entire system.

But the truth is that merely being invested enough in a centralized system is a major security risk. But it is a risk that is perfectly avoidable. When using blockchain technology, be sure to use platforms that are decentralized. Or, if you must use a centralized system, use it as little as possible.

Chapter 5: Potential Applications

In this chapter, we'll look at different sectors of business and areas of government and public service that might make use of the blockchain.

Business And Supply Chains

The business sector provides several opportunities for the use of blockchains. Trade typically involves getting approvals from several different entities in sequence, but with a blockchain, this could be done in such a way that the approvals occur all at once, and in such a way that any one participant could check on the status of the other approvals.

Supply chains are another area in which blockchains may prove useful. When part of a system or a machine fails, currently some entity must investigate errors and persuade each manufacturer and regulating body to provide information about what went wrong -- that is, to persuade them to reveal private information that should be public.

Not only must someone persuade possibly reluctant organizations to participate in the investigation, they must also find the source of the problem. Blockchains provide provenance, which can increase trust before an error occurs by ensuring that the relevant information about the supply chain is shared, and by ensuring that no one entity owns or restricts information that should be public in the first place.

Finance And Accounting

For accountants, blockchain technology may prove beneficial. For one thing, accounting usually requires records to be kept for a certain amount of time, and the blockchain can keep immutable records permanently. Furthermore, if the blockchain is adopted by both accountants and their clients, accountants will be able to manage their clients' accounts in real time. If people are using blockchain-based cryptocurrencies, a constantly updated ledger means that accountants can continuously observe the transactions as they occur, and the fact that the ledger is a comprehensive history of all relevant transactions means that auditing will be much easier.

Furthermore, the monthly accounting cycle may become a thing of the past. If the world is making instantaneous transactions, accountants will have to keep up. But this faster cycle will result in less pressure, not more, as the blockchain will automate most of the work.

Insurance

Insurance companies could use a blockchain to automate insurance claims in a way that would benefit both the insurance companies and their customers. The companies would save money by reducing the work that must be done by insurance agents, who at the moment have to closely scrutinize insurance claims and compare them against insurance policies. The work done by insurance agents could be replaced with automated smart contracts, which would automatically execute when someone qualifies for insurance. The blockchain could also prevent insurance fraud by making it easier to cross-reference insurance claims with factual data both internal and external to the blockchain.

Meanwhile, claimants would benefit from more efficient insurance payouts, get an estimate, and receive what they are owed more quickly. The blockchain can also increase trust in the insurance industry by promoting transparency. Bernard Marr wrote in a blog post titled "Blockchain Implications Every Insurance Company Needs To Consider Now" that "There's a crisis of trust in the financial services industry. Even though the large banks are the focal point, the erosion of trust impacts all businesses. Lack of trust, high costs and inefficiency of the insurance industry all play a part in the extraordinary high levels of underinsurance."

People will be able to investigate exactly why their claim was approved or denied, find out which insurance policies are truly worth investing in, find out which policies they aren't being told about, and find out when a relative's life insurance policy goes unclaimed.

Government Organizations

There are countless uses for the blockchain in government and public service. The spending habits of government organizations are just one. To take just one example, Canada's National Research Council (NRC) is trialing an Ethereum-based tool to publish information about funding and grants. Anyone can browse the database of grants at <u>explorecatena.com</u>, giving citizens total transparent access to the NRC's recent spending history, a practice that could expand to other areas of government.

But that's just one area of government that the blockchain is useful in; next we'll look at voting, identification, and land registration.

Voting And Identification

Identification is another application for blockchain technology. Currently, governments spend a lot of time and money verifying identification and trying to detect forgeries. Blockchains can solve this problem by replacing the need for people to inspect and judge physical IDs; instead, various pieces of unforgeable, timestamped data can serve as an ID. This would be especially useful in creating a secure electronic voting system that identifies voters by pulling in all sorts of data, without the inefficiencies that manual inspection involves, and without the security risks that other electronic voting systems would have.

Furthermore, some identification documents required by organizations may not be equally available to everyone. For example, banks may ask for electricity bills as an identifying document when you open a bank account, but people who have recently moved from another country may not have those documents. Instead of having a list of acceptable identifying documents, blockchains that can aggregate information can provide identifying data in such a way that is instantaneous and more versatile.

Land Registration

Various countries, including the U.K., Sweden, and the Ukraine, are testing or using the blockchain for land registration. Currently, if you want to buy property, you have to find the title and have it signed over by the owner. However, there are problems with the current system of documentation -- it is unreliable and prone to errors and forgery. But a blockchain that serves as a comprehensive catalogue could allow for easier and faster exchanges of land.

Non-Profit Organizations
When you donate to a charity, you don't get to directly see where your money goes. The organization always decides how to spend it, and may even spend some of it on its own members, or lose much of it to the cost of doing business.

But in a blockchain, it's possible to at the very least see who and what your investment is spent on, and even possible to transmit money directly to people in need. Recently, the United Nations World Food Programme used Ethereum to transfer vouchers for food directly to ten thousand refugees in Syria.

Medical Records

Medical records are another area where blockchains may be put to use. At present, patient medical data is sensitive information that requires manual authorization to be shared between hospitals, insurance and coverage providers, and doctors' offices. With a blockchain, a complete medical history could be held by each patient, and the blockchain could automatically grant access to certain individuals.

Chapter 6: Blockchain Projects

Smart Contracts

Smart contracts are contracts that are programmed with the blockchain that automatically execute when a certain event occurs. They remove the need for a third party to oversee the transaction at the moment it occurs.

Basically, there is no need for a middleman in smart contracts. A blockchain is simply a ledger that may need eventual oversight before anything more complex than a single transaction is done, but smart contracts are an extension of the blockchain that can independently enforce rules before an actual person ever takes action.

Smart contracts are commonly associated with Ethereum, but they are becoming increasingly commonplace and are a feature of many blockchains. Barclay's Corporate Bank, for example, has a series of templates that can be used to translate human-readable contracts from plain English into machine-readable smart contracts. These smart contracts retrieve information from external sources and automate account activity. The smart contracts also point to the original relevant document in case a person does need to involve themselves. Currently, the technology is being tested on interest rate swaps.

Data Storage

Data storage on the blockchain is currently a niche use, but has a lot of potential. Currently, most data is stored on centralized, dedicated servers, which cost a lot of money to run and maintain, and allow the provider to delete your data arbitrarily. To understand this, think of tools like Dropbox or Google Drive, which use dedicated servers to let users store data on the cloud.

By comparison, **Storj** is a peer to peer cloud storage site in which users store their data on peer computers on the network (or "nodes"). Instead of storing data on a dedicated server and trusting a company with their data, Storj allows any computer on the Internet to store data, and users are ensured that their data is private thanks to the blockchain's encryption features. Plus, participants who store data are rewarded with tokens that can be traded.

Crowd Sales

Crowdselling is similar to crowdfunding in that it involves raising money for a business or project. But whereas in crowdfunding, you would ask for money and give out merchandise or, say, list donors in the credits, crowdselling involves blockchain-based rewards. In crowdselling, you raise money by selling tokens which can eventually be redeemed. Of course, this is a risk for investors. But the tokens are tied to the expected and actual success of the project, so they have an instantly tradeable value that merchandise from the project does not have. In other words, your donors can have something that they can own or trade long before your project is completed.

Sharing Economy

The term "sharing economy" describes platforms and businesses, such as Uber and Airbnb, in which peers or contractors provide a service that the platform in question facilitates. In other words, there are technically no front-line employees. With a comprehensive enough blockchain, you could automatically identify and give certain participants permission to access certain things that you own -- for example, you could grant access to the devices in your guest cottage or the locks on your car's passenger door.

MyBit, for example, is a startup that deals in solar panels. Currently, most solar grids are large-scale, but there is the potential for people to have personal "microgrids" on their rooftops and in their yards. MyBit is a solution that allows people to monetize the surplus energy they produce. The blockchain allows people to own solar devices and authenticate other people's access to the panels. It does this by allowing owners of solar panels to sell surplus power that they produce for tokens, and by allowing other participants to buy surplus power from them.

Decentralized Internet

There are currently several ongoing attempts, such as the **Beaker** browser, to create a decentralized Internet on the blockchain. These applications rely on individual peers or nodes to act as peer-to-peer Internet servers, and they make use of the blockchain to ensure that the pages are authentic. This type of network has the benefit of being both uncensorable and resistant to downtime, because if it is widely used, there will always be a peer to serve you.

This goes hand in hand with attempts to build a decentralized peer to peer Internet infrastructure from nothing more than each user's hardware. Rather than relying on a city's Internet infrastructure, users could run a network on their wireless hardware. Just a few peers would need to rely on an internet service provider, and could serve the Internet to their peers wirelessly. Internet prices would be reduced, and users could compensate the peers who provide the Internet service with tokens. **Andrena** is one effort to accomplish something like this.

Online Dating

Online dating sites are a novel use for the blockchain. In typical dating sites, female users either receive too much attention from male users, or the dating sites charge a prohibitive subscription fee that discourages men from sending too many messages.

Luna is an upcoming blockchain-based dating site. On Luna, female users are paid in tokens once they respond to a message; male users pay to have their messages ranked more highly in a female user's inbox. In Luna, users hold tokens that have an actual value (the tokens can be exchanged for other currencies in addition to being used on the site) but administrators control how the tokens work on the dating site.

Chapter 7: Blockchain Security

In this chapter, we'll examine blockchain security. We've spent a lot of time examining the benefits of the blockchain, so we'll glance over those advantages only briefly. We'll spend more time on security issues and how to confront and avoid them. Topics include 51% attacks, inadvertent centralization, and keeping physical assets safe.

Plus we'll cover the typical issues faced by small networks, and see how difficult it is to test systems ahead of time. Most of this chapter is aimed at people implementing a blockchain, but this chapter will also briefly cover the risks that individual users face.

Advantages Over Current Technology
An ideal blockchain has several advantages in terms of security that current technology doesn't. It's much more difficult to hack and steal money or sensitive information from a blockchain, because the blockchain doesn't centralize information or ownership like banks

and other entities do. So a good blockchain will be secure against certain types of attacks such as counterfeiting and fraud. (Although blockchains are susceptible to certain attacks, like double spending and 51% attacks, which we'll look at in the next section).

The blockchain also has excellent integrity, as the blockchain platform and network are constantly check for errors, tampering, and other improper changes, whereas current networks require manual oversight and auditing to detect tampering. This means blockchains can resolve attacks almost immediately, which saves the cost of having to compensate participants after an attack is carried out.

The blockchain also provides security to individuals. It doesn't require individuals to trust an authority with their private information, and furthermore, it is uncensorable. It's also typically open and pseudonymous (although it can be designed otherwise), which means that the participants are protected from censorship and legal and political restrictions; participants can't be linked to a real identity that might prohibit them from participating in traditional systems (for example, the blockchain would allow payment from people who are not old enough to own a credit card, or people residing in countries that are not allowed to trade with each other). Participants can be identified only as far as security of the blockchain is concerned.

However, all these advantages over current systems also have downsides and limit security in certain ways, and we will look at these over the course of the chapter.

Vulnerabilities Of Blockchains

Blockchains are not perfectly secure. They are simply more secure than traditional systems in the best cases. In any traditional system, large amounts of money or sensitive information can be stolen, either by a malicious external actor, or by internal corruption amongst trusted members -- and it only takes a single attack on one powerful part of the system for disaster to strike. Participants with powerful privileges usually have control over most or all of the assets in the system, and only one needs to be compromised to bring down a centralized system.

Even though it is possible to hack, steal from, or otherwise compromise a blockchain, an attacker cannot simply do this by circumventing the security of one or a few authorities -- the attacker must have significant control over the participants and control over the process of reaching a consensus. Needless to say, it is far more difficult to gain control over several participants all using the same security measures than it is to compromise just one authority.

51% Attacks

That said, security breaches do occur sometimes, and a typical attack is a type called a 51% attack, which means that when a participant controls over 51% of a network, they have a very likely chance of tampering with the blockchain and getting away with it -- since they control most of the network, they can effectively dictate the consensus.

Exit Scams

Exit scams are another type of attack that occurs often, in which new blockchain startups are created just to get investments, before disappearing without a trace, taking the invested money with them. This is not really a risk if you are running a blockchain for your own organization, but it is a risk if you are investing in one, particularly if it is one that involves cryptocurrency. For this reason, it's important to use established cryptocurrencies, and to invest in young cryptocurrencies only if there are identifiable, reputable people behind them.

Inadvertent Centralization

Another unfortunate fact is that security is partly dictated by the users of the blockchain. A blockchain's security may be excellent, but it is powerless to stop its weakest participants from transferring their assets to a centralized system like an online wallet or a centralized exchange. In other words, blockchains and cryptocurrencies are frequently subject to attacks, but often the attack is not on the blockchain itself.

Often these attacks occur because a third party has gathered large amounts of a cryptocurrency or assets, and is storing them on their users' behalf. If a blockchain is valuable enough, it attracts a lot of investment, and it may be very attractive to users who use it carelessly and collectively allow large amounts to be held centrally by an online exchange or online wallet. The Mt. Gox exchange is an infamous case of a centralized exchange that was hacked, resulting in the theft of millions of dollars worth of Bitcoin.

In addition, even the assets in pure blockchains can be centralized in a sense. Ripple is one example of a cryptocurrency that operates on a blockchain, but it is also true that large amounts of Ripple are owned by a few founders and large companies like Microsoft. This makes it more attractive to banks and other traditional organizations.

However, because of the unique way that Ripple records debits, credits, and money owed, certain wallets act as sorts of banks, or "gateways," that the Ripple blockchain is semi-dependent on. "Around 50,000 wallets are highly vulnerable to disruption by as few as 10 wallets (…) and their credit with the gateways (a total of 14,338,105 USD) is at risk," according to Pedro Moreno-Sanchez et al. in "Mind Your Credit: Assessing the Health of the Ripple Credit Network." If these nodes go down or are compromised by an attack, a lot of assets stand to be lost.

However, Ripple has not been subject to a security breach of this type yet, and the blockchain may very well be secure enough to prevent an attack.

Lack of Privacy

Ideal blockchains are private. But due to the fact that your identity on the blockchain is only pseudonymous, if you use the blockchain enough, people may be able to analyze the patterns of your transactions and behavior and make inferences about your real-world identity based on who you make transactions with and how much stake you have in the blockchain.

One solution is to seek out blockchains that provide true anonymity. Monero is one cryptocurrency that tries to solve this by providing true built-in anonymity built into its blockchain. The more practical solution is to use a different identification (or "public address") for each transaction.

However, total privacy may not be possible -- and may even be irrelevant or undesirable -- in a business environment on an organization's own blockchain, in which the identities of participants are deliberately linked with real-world identities. There is a larger problem of choosing exactly what information should and should not be made private, and there is no answer that fits the needs of all scenarios.

For example, imagine you have an "employee of the month" program which, each time it is won, provides 10 credits to an employee on the blockchain. If everyone knows Bob has won 6 times, then they might infer that someone who earned 60 credits is Bob, even though "winning employee of the month" isn't personally identifying information as we normally think of it. Now everyone knows which previously anonymous blockchain participant is Bob. This becomes a serious problem if you also want to implement, say, an anonymous suggestion box on the same blockchain that the employee of the month program is running on.

Unfortunately, the bottom line is that for any blockchain, at least some information must *not* be private, and developers must decide how to work with that.

Security Of Physical Assets

It is one thing to make a cryptocurrency transaction irreversible and permanent, as the assets (ie. the tokens) are entirely virtual. They cannot be stolen unless someone is participating in the blockchain, and if they are, they are subject to the same security measures that everyone else is.

On the other hand, if transactions on your blockchain describe physical goods in the real world, the fact that those records are irreversible and permanent will not dictate the actual behavior of people with access to those goods. If a thief has physical access to your goods, a blockchain is hardly likely to stop them from stealing those goods.

This raises the question of whether, and to what extent, you can force people to participate in your blockchain, and to what extent you are simply enforcing rules that you would have to implement without the blockchain. Be sure that you are not just using a blockchain as a high-tech, but easily circumvented, lock.

Small Networks

A blockchain relies on its users and nodes, and it will typically reach a critical point where it is secure because it has enough participants. However, the smaller a blockchain is, the more vulnerable it is to attacks: a single participant can gain relatively more power in the early stages of a blockchain's growth, leaving it more prone to a 51% attack in which the attacker controls the consensus.

And small distributed networks are also vulnerable to total inactivity and can become "dead" networks. Although this is not a matter of security per se, it is a risk. A robust blockchain is always available, but blockchains that are still in their early stages can collapse.

Bisq (formerly known as Bitsquare) is one example of this challenge. It is a decentralized exchange where the administrators do not own large reserves of cryptocurrency on their users' behalf, and peers merely serve as temporary trusted escrow agents that can hold a transaction until both parties are satisfied. Bisq is much more secure than (and has far lower fees than) centralized exchanges, but at the moment it struggles to provide peers; finding someone to trade with can be very difficult.

Lack Of Testing And Review

If you are building a blockchain, it will at some point come time to test it. Since blockchains typically involve assets with considerable value, this is no small feat. Case in point: The DAO was the first decentralized autonomous organization. It was built on Ethereum, and although people involved in its development raised a concern, nothing was done to fix those issues, and The

DAO was hacked. $55 million worth of Ether was stolen directly from the blockchain.

There are inherent difficulties in implementing tests, though. Blockchains are meant to have the potential to be scaled up, and it is hard to test a blockchain at full scale during development. The two most important steps one can take is to have the code peer-reviewed, and to have smart contracts tested by independent entities.

Individual Security
Even if a blockchain remains secure, it can provide poor security for its users. All it takes for a user to lose what they own and control is to take no precaution in securing their private information. All one has to do to compromise one's individual security is store their private keys in a public place -- or have those keys stolen due to insufficient security measures.

There are preventative measures one can take against theft. One is two-factor authentication, in which private information is kept under a second layer of encryption. Another precaution is cold storage, in which you store your private information on a dedicated offline system or even on a piece of paper. But these precautions are not typically built into the blockchain, and are the responsibility of the participants.

Although theft and the loss of private information is a problem of traditional systems as well, current systems like banks and credit card companies may sometimes provide recourse or compensation -- whereas in a blockchain there is likely no compensation for the attacks an individual suffers.

Chapter 8: Future Of The Blockchain

In this chapter, we'll look at the blockchain's future and learn how it will evolve from its current use, which is primarily within the cryptocurrency market. We'll see how blockchains will change business practices by promoting fair competition, and how blockchains will change society by creating a worldwide economy that is easy to participate in.

Bitcoin

Cryptocurrency is currently one of the most frequent uses of blockchain technology, and we can look to it to see what challenges blockchains will face in general. Bitcoin was the very first application of the blockchain. It's a decentralized, blockchain-based cryptocurrency. Much of Bitcoin's appeal is in the fact that it's more flexible and freely usable than nearly any system that came before it. There is no need for banks when using

Bitcoin -- anyone can be on either end of a Bitcoin transaction.

It is only the beginning of cryptocurrencies, though. Bitcoin has drawbacks, such as long transaction times and high fees that simply did not scale as Bitcoin gained popularity and value. Bitcoin is also not truly anonymous, just pseudonymous -- users aren't identified, but since the ledger is open to scrutiny, anyone can see which addresses have performed transactions, meaning that participants must constantly take on new identities if they want to remain anonymous. And although it has grown in value more than any other cryptocurrency that came after it, competing cryptocurrencies have began to take up more and more of the market.

It's also difficult to exchange cryptocurrencies for non-cryptocurrency funds. Many countries tax cryptocurrency even before it is changed into fiat currency. Banks can stop transactions related to cryptocurrency at their discretion. China has recently shut down cryptocurrency exchanges. It's not all bad news; Paypal has started accepting Bitcoin in their transactions. There is certainly a future for cryptocurrency, but what exactly that future will look like is anyone's guess.

In short, businesses that use the blockchain will need to solve the same problems that cryptocurrencies have: the delicate balance of private and public information; how to grow the value of a niche token in the face of competing blockchain technologies; and how to make the blockchain work in conjunction with centralized organizations.

Changes In Business

Blockchains will mainly reduce the costs needed to administrate your typical business interactions by removing the need for highly paid, privileged administrators and auditors. Currently, highly trusted figures are paid highly so as to make corruption and fraud not worthwhile to engage in -- yet sometimes they are nevertheless prone to corruption. The blockchain can solve this problem by replacing these positions with a self-administering system that is audited by the participants.

Furthermore, in a market, entire organizations can engage in collusion and anti-competition activities through the formation of cartels and monopolies. Currently, there are laws that disincentivize anti-competitive activities, although participants can still break the rules and defect from the law. Ideally, a blockchain could prevent this from happening by virtue of being a system that only works when rules are abided by. In other words, businesses would not have to worry about whether their competitors are abiding by the rules, because they could see the actions of those competitors. This would also be of benefit to customers by doubling as consumer protection.

However, there are overhead costs when it comes to doing business with the blockchain. On a small scale, you will at minimum have to ensure that your participants have access to computers to actually participate (though they do not necessarily need to own one). You'll have to also make sure that you employ people and attract customers who are willing or incentivized to participate in your blockchain, though once established and adopted, blockchain solutions will probably be cheaper than current systems.

Changes In Society

Blockchains mean that anyone can be on the other end of a transaction, depending on how open the people participating in the blockchain decide to make it. For example, people in developing countries usually have internet access at far greater rates than they have access to bank accounts. This lets anyone participate in a worldwide economy unhampered by physical distance.

Take an alternative like Paypal, for example, in which a centralized company transfers money and can make arbitrary decisions. Paypal can temporarily suspend an account, take extra fees from international transfers, or decide to let someone unilaterally reverse their payment -- all at their discretion, leaving you to negotiate with Paypal. Paypal is also able to prevent users under certain ages from withdrawing money to their bank account, and Paypal is entirely unavailable in several countries.

But with a cryptocurrency based on a blockchain, whether the participant is a person who doesn't have access to a bank account, or a device that has been programmed to autonomously participate in blockchain transactions, you can carry out that transaction without the possibility of a central authority deciding to restrict the transaction. Blockchains remove the need for middlemen like Paypal.

Inexpensive blockchain-based business models will also increase competition, producing better products and services for people. Consider the case of Napster, a music sharing service that existed in the early 2000s. Napster was able to compete with distributors of music by providing a protocol for peer-to-peer music sharing. Although it broke copyright law, it was nevertheless a technical feat that the proper distributors of music simply couldn't accomplish. By creating a distributed system that put the responsibility to distribute music on the shoulders of users, Napster reduced the cost of distribution dramatically to the point that users were willing to run a distribution network for free.

Napster was eventually shut down because it broke the law, but decentralized music piracy continues to be something that is inexpensive, but that the music industry has trouble competing with and monetizing. Meanwhile, the music industry has successfully been able to monetize music piracy on centralized websites like YouTube by relying on ad revenue. The main difference is that YouTube can negotiate with artists and uploaders, something that the blockchain can also do, but that Napster could not.

One can imagine that a blockchain might one day be used by the music industry to both prevent piracy and to get people to distribute music on their behalf by providing them with a tokenized royalty incentive to share music, while also providing an incentive to abide by the rules that they set out. Lance Koonce, an intellectual property lawyer, in an article for Big Law Business, writes that "the idea of media files living in the wild, outside of the owner's immediate immediate control, might initially fill industry veterans with fear. However, the aspects of blockchain technology that provide transaction transparency and security also offer the possibility of more robust access control, and better tracking of infringement when it does occur."

And that's just one example. More broadly, blockchain technology allows the possibility of an economy and ecosystem of content that anyone can participate in -- or on a smaller scale, that anyone in your organization can participate in.

Chapter 9: Blockchain Platforms

So you want to develop a blockchain? Now we are ready to look at various tools you can use. Keep in mind that most of these tools are targeted at developers, not at general users. If you decide to use one of these tools, remember to take into consideration the platform's frontend for end users as well as it's features for developers.

Note that many of the platforms in this chapter will use a **federation-based** or **voting-based** consensus mechanism, which simply involve trusted members with special permissions collectively deciding which version of the blockchain to use. This mechanism is neither proof of stake nor proof of work. It's ideal for businesses, organizations, and other closed systems with high levels of trust because it doesn't require you to rely on computers solving an algorithm, which is costly and time consuming.

Docker

Tagline: "Docker is an open platform for developers and sysadmins to build, ship, and run distributed applications, whether on laptops, data center VMs, or the cloud"

Docker is not a blockchain in and of itself. Instead, it is a tool that facilitates the installation of distributed applications such as blockchain platforms. Dockerhub is a website that is a repository of applications that contains many of the blockchain applications listed below. It could be said to be the Google Play store of web development. If you are in doubt as to how to install any of the software in this section, search the Docker Hub repository at hub.docker.com, and you may be able to get a simplified installation procedure.

Hyperledger
Tagline: "Hyperledger is an open source collaborative effort created to advance cross-industry blockchain technologies. It is a global collaboration, hosted by The Linux Foundation, including leaders in finance, banking, Internet of Things, supply chains, manufacturing and Technology."

Hyperledger Fabric was created by the Linux Foundation and IBM for the purpose of developing blockchains. One major selling point for some developers is that it doesn't rely on a cryptocurrency -- so you do not have to worry about mining or computational power as a means of reaching a consensus. Consensus is achieved when the policies defined in the ledger are met. You can find Hyperledger Fabric on Docker Hub if you want to host it yourself. Alternately, **IBM Blockchain on Bluemix** allows you to use a remote version hosted on the cloud.

Other versions of Hyperledger also exist. **Hyperledger Iroha** is a variant of Hyperledger targeted at mobile development. **Hyperledger Sawtooth Lake** is a variant intended for developing both permissioned and permissionless blockchains, and it uses a proof of elapsed time consensus mechanism, which is very efficient on Intel processors.

Ethereum

Tagline: "Ethereum is a decentralized platform for applications that run exactly as programmed without any chance of fraud, censorship or third-party interference. These apps run on a custom built blockchain, an enormously powerful shared global infrastructure that can move value around and represent the ownership of property."

Ethereum is a cryptocurrency and blockchain platform that can be used to develop and run smart contracts. It allows you to build your own blockchain applications or dApps. Consensus is reached through proof of work, namely Ethash mining. It's extremely popular, and a good choice if you are even slightly interested in dealing with established cryptocurrencies and do not mind outsourcing computer power (ie. relying on mining) as a consensus mechanism.

You will run your own blockchain, and there are multiple pieces of software you'll need to accomplish this, so the Ethereum setup process is somewhat more complex than the setup of other platforms. Documentation is available on the Ethereum website. An easy to use snapshot is also available from Docker.

HydraChain

Tagline: "HydraChain is an extension of the Ethereum platform which adds support for creating Permissioned Distributed Ledgers. Its primary domain of application are private chain or consortium chain setups."

HydraChain is another platform that is compatible with Ethereum. Instead of proof of work, accountable validators with special permissions dictate and negotiate consensus. This consensus mechanism also makes the consensus very fast, and prevents forking and reversals. HydraChain supports smart contracts both developed in Python and developed for the Ethereum platform. HydraChain is a good choice if you want to use Ethereum, but don't want to depend on Ethereum's slow and costly mining and proof of work consensus.

Monax (Eris:db)

Tagline: "The monax platform is an open platform for developers and devops to build, ship, and run blockchain-based applications for business ecosystems. Monax sells legally compliant smart contract-based SDKs to accelerate your time to market with sophisticated ecosystem applications."

Monax, formerly **Eris:db** is a permissioned blockchain platform that runs smart contracts. It also provides Ethereum support via a virtual machine, which means it can run both its own smart contracts and those developed for Ethereum. It uses a form of proof of stake consensus called Tendermint. The product is free, but Monax also sells support and instruction, so it's a good choice if you want dedicated help setting up a blockchain.

Quorum And Cakeshop

Tagline: "Quorum is an enterprise-focused version of Ethereum.Quorum is ideal for any application requiring high speed and high throughput processing of private transactions within a permissioned group of known participants. Quorum addresses specific challenges to blockchain technology adoption within the financial industry, and beyond."

Quorum is yet another distributed ledger based on Ethereum. It is used to develop smart contracts targeted at enterprises. Quorum uses a Raft-based consensus mechanism, which is complicated, but suffice to say, it is a faster and less costly alternative to Ethereum's proof of work. This makes Quorum applicable in secure, closed settings such as businesses, much like HydraChain.

Quora is noteworthy for being developed by the financial services company JP Morgan. It claims that it only minimally deviates from Ethereum's code. It also has one very useful feature: it offers a graphic interface called **Cakeshop**, which may make it easier for non-programmers to develop smart contracts. Both products are free.

Waves
Tagline: "Use blockchain -- it's easy with Waves. Issue, store, manage, trade, and analyze your digital assets safely with Waves blockchain platform and decentralized exchange."

Waves is a blockchain platform for cryptocurrency tokens. Like Ethereum, Waves provides a platform for developing smart contracts, but puts it front and center: Waves is unique in that it provides a platform for smart contracts built into its core wallet. It has an offline client, and an online client is still in Beta. However, it has an API that you can use with any client you develop yourself.

Waves has a proof of stake consensus mechanism. Participants are rewarded with commissions from their transactions, and transaction fees are low. All of this means that Waves is a good choice if you're working primarily with cryptocurrencies.

BigChainDB

Tagline: "BigchainDB allows developers and enterprise to deploy blockchain proof-of-concepts, platforms and applications with a scalable blockchain database, supporting a wide range of industries and use cases."

BigchainDB is an open-source blockchain platform that is meant to be a very fast database for very large amounts of data. Like Hyperledger, it doesn't have a built-in cryptocurrency; however, it does support various tokens and currencies. It also supports public and private networks, and offers fine control over user permissions. It uses a federation (ie. a voting-based) consensus mechanism, which makes it good for high-trust business settings.

BigChainDB is a good choice if you are used to managing databases; that is, ideal if you want a database first and a blockchain ledger second. It offers a web client that will manage the setup of the platform for you, and you can also install your own locally-hosted BigChainDB server with Docker.

Chain Core

Tagline: "Using Chain Core, institutions can launch and operate a blockchain network, or connect to a growing list of other networks that are transforming how assets move around the world."

Chain Core is meant to be used to transfer financial assets. It is notable for being backed by VISA. There is a free Developer edition and a paid Enterprise edition. Chain Core supports permission management and multi-signature technology. It uses a federation-based consensus mechanism. It's a good choice if you want to handle not just money, but also things with value like securities, gift cards, tokens, and points.

Like most blockchain platforms, it features native digital assets and smart contracts. Unlike most blockchains, it also features total privacy, meaning that only those involved in a transaction can see details. This means that Chain Core is a good choice if you're used to traditional transactions.

Chain Core must be installed locally, although you can deploy it to the cloud. It is also available on Docker.

Corda

Tagline: "Corda is a distributed ledger platform designed to record, manage and automate legal agreements between business partners. Designed by (and for) the world's largest financial institutions yet with applications in multiple industries. It offers a unique response to the privacy and scalability challenges facing decentralised applications."

Corda is yet another open-source ledger system. It features pluggable consensus, which means that you can choose from various modes of consensus. It is a good choice if you like a lot of control over the tools you use and need to access external data sources. It supports smart contracts and dApps ("CorDapps"), and these can be programmed with Java. An image is available on Docker Hub.

Credits

Tagline: "CREDITS is an open blockchain platform with autonomous smart contracts and the internal cryptocurrency. The platform is designed to create services for blockchain systems using self-executing smart contracts and a public data registry."

Credits is another framework for distributed ledgers. It uses a proof of stake consensus mechanism, which means that different participants get different amounts of votes when it comes to resolving versions of the ledger. It's very fast, has low transaction fees, and can be used to develop smart contracts. It boasts that it can be run completely autonomously without input from participants. It's a good choice if you want to work with a system with its own cryptocurrency, but want one that is more experimental than Ethereum.

Domus Tower Blockchain

Tagline: "Domus combines deep blockchain encryption and network expertise with Wall Street experience and a strong regulatory foundation."

Domus Tower Blockchain is a tool that's targeted at small groups dealing with finances. It allows linked blockchains where assets match liabilities, and balance sheets that track debits and credits. Instead of a true consensus mechanism, Domus Tower Blockchain simply allows you to give write permissions to any user, so a single person can determine the blockchain independently. It's a good choice if you work in a group where everyone knows each other and/or a high-trust environment. Domus Tower can be obtained by contacting the development team for a custom enterprise solution.

Elements Blockchain

Tagline: "A collection of feature experiments and extensions to the Bitcoin protocol. This platform enables anyone to build their own businesses or networks involving sidechain pegged Bitcoin or arbitrary asset tokens."

Elements blockchain is a tool that is meant as an extension to Bitcoin. It essentially lets you run your own blockchain as part of Bitcoin. The features that it offers number too many to go into in depth here, but if you are familiar with Bitcoin development, Elements provides confidential assets and transactions, timelocked transactions, new opcodes, deterministic pegs for moving transactions between blockchains, signed blocks, and more. It's a good choice if you are very familiar with Bitcoin, but want more features.

Multichain

Tagline: An "open source private blockchain platform, backwards compatible with bitcoin and Bitcoin Core."

Multichain is a tool that enables the creation of public and permissioned blockchains. It's very simple, and doesn't require programming knowledge. It's a good choice if you need a simple tool to use across multiple platforms and want to install a small piece of software on each participant's machine rather than have a web server run the software.

There is a command-line interface and a web frontend available. Additionally, **Yobichain** is based on Multichain and provides extra tools, like a graphical frontend, as well as access via database, web, and FTP servers.

Openchain

Tagline: "Openchain is an open source distributed ledger technology. It is suited for organizations wishing to issue and manage digital assets in a robust, secure and scalable way."

Openchain is an open-source distributed ledger with several useful features. It has typical features, such as immutability, scalability, and transparency.

Additionally, it also has a hierarchy of accounts and permissions, and multiple levels of ledgers -- including a fully open and anonymous ledger, and a closed-loop ledger that requires approval from the administrators. You can also assign human-readable aliases to participants' long ID hashes. It operates on a partitioned consensus scheme, which means that the way that transactions are validated depends on what asset is involved in the transaction. It's a good choice if you want convenient features that are easy to understand and that you are likely to use.

Symbiont Assembly

Tagline: "A blockchain platform for building networks in which multiple, independent entities may share data and logic in real time. It is a decentralized database that replicates and executes application logic in the form of smart contracts...Assembly was purpose-built to meet the standards of institutional finance in security, reliability and performance."

Symbiont Assembly is an up-and-coming system for smart contracts, modelling complex business logic and workflows, and is meant for the storage of legal documents and large files. It's a good choice if you are familiar with Apache Kafka, which Symbiont

Assembly was inspired by, or if you need to store large amounts of data.

IOTA

Tagline: "IOTA enables companies to explore new business-2-business models by making every technological resource a potential service to be traded on an open market in real time, with no fees.

IOTA is a distributed ledger that is not a blockchain. It has a "tangle", or a network of blocks, which is technically called a Directed Acyclic Graph. Unlike in a blockchain, each block in IOTA is dependent on many other blocks, meaning that IOTA can be scaled up drastically. There are drawbacks, though; it's usefulness is largely dependent on wide adoption.

It does not yet have a smart contract feature or timestamp features, but these are planned. IOTA is not a practical solution at the moment, so there is not much you can do with IOTA yet except for invest in its tokens. It has good company; Canonical, the company behind the very popular Ubuntu Linux, has been working with IOTA to develop a way of micro-billing for telecommunications.

Conclusion

Now that we've reached the end of this book, it should be clear how blockchains work, what they can do for you, and how you can run one. The essential properties of the blockchain are that it is an immutable and distributed ledger, with each block linked to the one before it, and that it requires consensus amongst its participants. The blockchain helps to run contracts, carry out transactions, save money, make some information public, and correct and prevent errors.

The blockchain began with cryptocurrencies like Bitcoin, but it is now becoming more present with the arrival of dApps, decentralized autonomous organizations, and smart contracts. All these tools enable traditional business activities to be performed automatically, and promise to bring as many participants as possible into business activities. A blockchain can keep records, provide transparency, allow you to set permissions, and provide greater network uptime. All these features combine to make an incredibly open, robust, and accessible system.

There are more technical aspects that we covered. We examined what it means when a blockchain is distributed and decentralized -- that it is run on a peer to peer network made up the participants' systems, or "nodes", and that the most active participants with the most stake have a sort of vote in reaching a consensus and determining the valid version of a blockchain.

We also examined how ownership, security, and privacy features are facilitated, thanks to the division between public and private information and the use of hashes and permissions. We also saw the security pitfalls of blockchains, like 51% attacks, accidental centralization, necessarily reduced privacy, and the vulnerabilities of small networks.

We looked at business applications of blockchains and actual projects that are ongoing. The blockchain promises to be useful in areas of the economy such as business, trade, supply chains, accounting, and insurance. It also can be useful in areas of government, such as identification and funding and grants.

Finally, we saw a number of platforms that you can use, including but not limited to big names like Ethereum and IBM's Hyperledger. If there is just one takeaway, perhaps it is this: there is no limit to what you can do with a well-constructed blockchain.

www.ingramcontent.com/pod-product-compliance
Lightning Source LLC
Chambersburg PA
CBHW071101240526
45471CB00016B/2293